neighborhoods in nature™

Let's Take a Field Trip to a
Coral Reef

Kathy Furgang

The Rosen Publishing Group's
PowerKids Press™
New York

★ To Dad, for being a great teacher ★

Published in 2000 by The Rosen Publishing Group, Inc.
29 East 21st Street, New York, NY 10010

Photo Credits: pp. 4, 7 Wayne Green; p. 8 © Photo Researchers, © Superstock; p. 10 © Animals, Animals; p. 11 © Wayne Green; p. 12 © Photo Researchers, © Wayne Green, © Animals, Animals; p. 13 © Wayne Green, p. 14 © Photo Researchers, p. 15 © Wayne Green, © Animals, Animals; p. 16 © Wayne Green, © Photo Researchers, p. 17 © Photo Researchers; p. 18 © Photo Researchers, © Wayne Green; p. 19 © Wayne Green, pp. 20, 21 © Photo Researchers; pp. 22, 23 © Wayne Green

Photo Illustrations by Thaddeus Harden

First Edition

Book Design: Felicity Erwin

Furgang, Kathy.
    Let's take a field trip to a coral reef / by Kathy Furgang.
        p.   cm. — (Neighborhoods in nature)
    Includes index.
    Summary: Explains the nature of a coral reef, the conditions it needs to grow, and the plant and animal life surrounding it.
    ISBN 0-8239-5445-5 (lib. bdg.)
    1. Coral reef ecology—Juvenile literature. [1. Coral reefs and islands. 2. Coral reef ecology. 3. Ecology.] I. Title. II. Series: Furgang, Kathy. Neighborhoods in nature.
    QH541.5.C7 F87 1999
    577.7'89—dc21

                                                                        98-53285
                                                                            CIP
                                                                            AC

Contents

What is Coral?

Coral is an amazing underwater **community** made up of sea creatures that are both living and dead. These tiny sea creatures are called **polyps**. Polyps come in different colors and sizes. They look like branches of trees, or tiny pipes and tubes. Many people mistake coral for a plant because of the way the polyps look.

Coral is formed in the ocean when polyps die. Millions of polyp skeletons turn into a hard rock, called **limestone**. Coral gets bigger when new, live polyps attach themselves to the limestone. Polyps live and grow on top of the skeletons of their dead relatives!

◀ *When polyps die, they later become coral for other polyps to settle and live on. This makes coral grow larger and larger.*

How are Coral Reefs Formed?

Parts of coral are living and parts of it are dead. The limestone skeletons, or dead polyps, stay attached to the ocean floor, and new polyps keep growing on top of them. New polyps attach themselves to the coral and make the coral grow larger. This growing goes on for hundreds, even thousands, of years. When coral grows in a shallow area of the ocean over many years, it can grow above the level of the ocean water. The part of the coral that grows above water becomes an island known as a **coral reef**.

Different sea plants grow close to coral, so many animals, like long spine squirrelfish and yellow finger sponge, make their homes there, too. ▶

Long Spine Squirrelfish

Yellow Finger Sponge

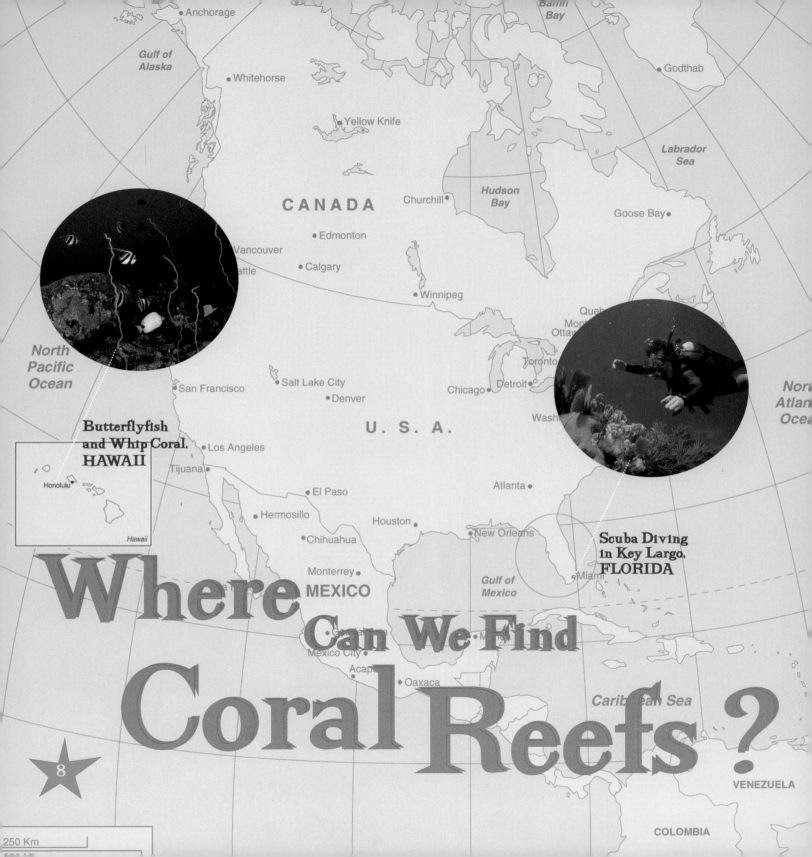

Butterflyfish
and Whip Coral,
HAWAII

Honolulu

Hawaii

Scuba Diving
in Key Largo,
FLORIDA

Where Can We Find Coral Reefs?

250 Km

VENEZUELA

COLOMBIA

Coral grows in all oceans. Coral reefs, however, only form under special conditions. The ocean water must be:

★ no more than 150 feet deep, so that the coral can eventually grow above water. (This is about as high as a 10-story building.)

★ in a **tropical** area, which means that the area stays hot all year long

★ clean, so that sunlight can shine through the water and help the coral grow

★ always moving, so that the ocean waves can carry food to the polyps

Coral reefs form over thousands of years when all these conditions are met.

◀ *In the United States, coral reefs can be found in the ocean waters of Florida and Hawaii.*

How Polyps Find Food

There are many plants and sea creatures living near coral that the coral polyps can eat. Polyps cannot swim. They cannot even move very much, so they count on the moving ocean water to carry food to them. Polyps eat a lot of **algae**. Algae are simple, tiny creatures made up of only one cell. Polyps also eat fish, worms, and other small sea animals. When the animal is close enough to touch, the polyp stings it with its feelers. The feelers have poison in them that makes the animal unable to move. While the animal is still, the polyp sucks it into its mouth.

◀ *Don't get too close to coral! The polyps sting. If a human touches coral by accident, the sting can hurt.*

11

Neighborhoods Below Water

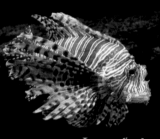

Lionfish

Purple Tube Sponge

Clownfish

Starfish

◀ Some fish in the coral reef community are:
- lionfish
- clownfish
- purple tube sponge
- blue sea starfish
- stoplight parrotfish

Fish that live around coral reefs have special features that help them live there. Many have slim bodies so they can swim through holes in the coral without being stung. Others have large fins so they can slide through the water smoothly without hitting the coral.

Coral makes a great home for beautiful sea creatures. Many fish in these tropical waters are brightly colored. Colors help fish to recognize each other and **communicate** with other fish. With their colors, they can send each other messages without using words. A clown fish knows that other clown fish are bright orange and white. Colors help fish to identify which fish are harmless and which might be dangerous.

Stoplight parrotfish

13

Neighborhoods Above Water

Mangrove Tree

Over thousands of years, coral reefs grow to reach the surface of the ocean. Communities of plants, animals, and birds make their home on the reefs, just above the water.

Roots of **mangrove trees** grow in coral, sand, and rock. Many of these trees grow out of coral that is covered in water. Mangrove trees have beautiful, twisted roots that look like branches coming out of the ocean. The leaves on the trees stay green all year long. These trees give shade and food to birds and animals.

Cormorant and Pelican

Egret

Lagoon Iguana

Life on a coral reef above ▶ the ocean water is just as interesting as the world of coral below.

Cormorants on Mangrove T

Christmas Tree Worms

Chromodorid Nudibranches

16

Birds like to hide in the branches and leaves of the mangrove trees and then swoop down to catch fish and animals in the water.

Animals at the Top

Finding food is not always easy for the animals who live on the coral reef. Worms, snails, shrimp, clams, oysters, and birds all make their homes on coral reefs near the surface of the ocean and need to find things to eat. They all feed on the leaves of mangrove trees that grow in the coral. Birds eat from the branches, and sea animals eat the leaves that fall into the water. Small creatures must be careful. Larger animals such as crabs, fish, and birds could eat them. Every creature in the community must find food.

Atoll

Lagoon

Some of the most beautiful animals in ▶
the world live underwater near
different kinds of coral reefs.

Fringing Reef

Different Kinds of Coral Reefs

There are several different kinds of coral reefs. A **barrier-type reef** grows in front of land to make a barrier, or block, between the ocean and the land. Barrier-type reefs create an area of calm water called a **lagoon**. A **fringing reef** spreads from the shore out into the sea. Fringing reefs are usually covered by water. An **atoll** is a round coral island in the open sea. Many people have discovered how beautiful all of these reefs are. In fact, some people even plan their vacations near the colorful coral to see the creatures that live there.

The Great Barrier Reef

The **Great Barrier Reef** in Australia is the largest coral reef in the world. It is more than 1,250 miles long and spreads off the northeastern coast of Queensland, Australia.

The Great Barrier Reef is in trouble. Since the 1960s, thousands more starfish than normal have been settling on the coral each year and eating the living polyps. These starfish are destroying the reef. Scientists have not yet been able to figure out why so many starfish settle there, or how to stop them from hurting the coral.

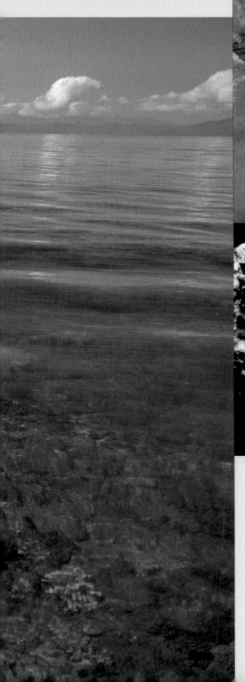

Having too many starfish on the coral reef disrupts the cycle of life. Coral is being destroyed faster than it is being made.

21

Coral Reefs are in Danger

Around the world, coral reef communities are being **damaged** and destroyed. People cut down mangrove trees to make shrimp farming easier. In Southeast Asia, over half of the mangroves have been destroyed in the past 15 years. If the mangrove trees are destroyed, then the small animals that get their food from these trees will die. When the small animals that are food for polyps are gone, the polyps and coral will die.

Scientists are determined to save these ocean communities and the animals that live there. They are working hard to save the coral reefs around the world.

Web Sites:

You can learn more about coral and coral reefs on the Internet. Check out at these Web sites:

www.hiwassee.edu/~nsf-coral/

www.seaworld.org/coral_reefs/coralcr.html

Glossary

algae (AL-jee) A plant without roots or stems that usually lives in water.

atoll (ATOHL) A round coral island in the sea.

barrier-type reef (BAYR-ee-ur TYP REEF) A coral reef that grows between the ocean and the land, and is separated from the land by a lagoon.

coral (KOR-ul) Many tiny animals, called polyps, attached to polyp skeletons.

coral reef (KOR-ul REEF) An island made of coral.

communicate (kuh-MYOO-nih-kayt) To share information or feelings.

community (kuh-MYOO-nih-tee) A group of people or animals that live in the same place.

damage (DAM-ij) To cause harm.

fringing reef (FRIN-jing REEF) A reef covered in water that spreads from land out to sea.

Great Barrier Reef (GRAYHT BAYR-ee-ur REEF) The largest coral reef in the world, found off the coast of Australia.

lagoon (la-GOON) A pond or small lake connected with a larger body of water.

limestone (LYM-stohn) A rock that is formed from shells and skeletons.

mangrove trees (MAHN-grohv TREEZ) Trees found on coral reefs.

polyps (PAH-lyps) Small animals that make up coral. They attach to the limestone section of coral.

tropical (TROH-pih-kuhl) When weather conditions are hot and moist year-round.

Index★